NUTRIBULLET RECIPES

Ashley Andrews

All rights Reserved. No part of this publication or the information in it may be quoted from or reproduced in any form by means such as printing, scanning, photocopying or otherwise without prior written permission of the copyright holder.

Disclaimer and Terms of Use: Effort has been made to ensure that the information in this book is accurate and complete, however, the author and the publisher do not warrant the accuracy of the information, text and graphics contained within the book due to the rapidly changing nature of science, research, known and unknown facts and internet. The Author and the publisher do not hold any responsibility for errors, omissions or contrary interpretation of the subject matter herein. This book is presented solely for motivational and informational purposes only.

Contents

Your Free Gift 1
Introduction 2
PREVENTION SMOOTHIES 4
Banana Ginger Smoothie 5
Orange Dream Creamsicle 6
Green Tea, Blueberry and Banana Smoothie 7
Very Berry Breakfast Smoothie 9
World's Best Smoothie 10
Pineapple Passion 11
Strawberry-Kiwi Smoothie 12
Banana-Blueberry-Soy (BBS) Smoothie 13
Tropical Papaya Perfection 14
Just Peachy 15
Apricot-Mango Madness 16
Watermelon Wonder 18
Berry Vanilla Sensation Smoothie 19
Tutti-Frutti Smoothie 20
Lucy's Luscious Smoothie 21
Slim-Down Smoothie 22
Soy, Soy Good Smoothie 23
Tropical Mango Madness Smoothie 24
SLIMMING SMOOTHIES 25
Mango Surprise Smoothie 26
Blueberry Smoothie 27
Bano-Peanut Butter Smoothie 28
Vanilla and Blueberry Smoothie 29
Just Peachy Smoothie 30

Citrusy Lemon-Orange Smoothie 31
Spicy Apple Smoothie 32
Tropicalicious Pineapple Smoothie 33
Strawberry Stunner Smoothie 34
DETOX SMOOTHIES 35
Limango Collard Green Smoothie 36
Hale to the Kale 37
Sweet Spirulina Smoothie 38
Chia Chiller Smoothie 39
Tangy Tummy Smoothie 40
Smooth Operator 41
Sexy Crazy Goddess 42
The Sicilian Smoothie 43
Lemon-Blueberry Smoothie 44
Gingery Blueberry 45
Apple Mint Berry Smoothie 46
Sensual Detox Smoothie 47
Lean Green Machine 48
Glowing NutriBlast 49
Warrior Tonic 50
Clear Skin Sip 51
The Fountain of Youth 52
Cranberry Cleanser 53
"Fat Flush" Juice 54
Simply Healthy 55
Peachy Watermelon Smoothie 56
Good Morning Green Smoothie 57
Winter Smoothie 59

Heart Healthy Smoothie..60
Minty Lemon and Honeydew Melon Smoothie 61
Nutmeg Spiced Honey Banana Smoothie...................................62
Spiced Pumpkin Smoothie..64
Other Books by the Author...65
Additional Resources..66

Your Free Gift

As a thank you for reading this book, I would like to give you a free gift. It includes several of my favorite juicing recipes and is a perfect complement to this book that will help you along your journey.

Visit http://www.deepthoughtpress.com/nutribullet/ to download your free gift.

All the best,

Ashley

Introduction

The NutriBullet is an amazing food extractor that not only creates great tasting food, but it also allows you to get the most health benefits out of the ingredients you use. This book will provide you with many healthy and great tasting smoothie recipes. The smoothies in this book are jam packed with minerals, vitamins, antioxidants, protein and dietary fiber. And best of all, they are extremely tasty.

In the coming pages you will discover a wide variety of smoothie recipes. One type of smoothie you'll see is a green smoothie and it usually consists of fresh fruit and dark, leafy greens like collards, spinach, chard, and kale. Bok Choy and Romaine are also great choices for green smoothies.

You'll also encounter some really creamy smoothies too. Using creamy fruits like banana, mango, kiwi and papaya provide that awesomely creamy texture for your smoothies. You can even use avocadoes, apples, berries, pears, peaches and pineapples.

You will also find a variety of liquid bases in the follow recipes. Coconut, almond, soy milk as well as yoghurt and milk can be used as a liquid base. For a health boost use chia, hemp and flax seeds, protein and acai powders, coconut oil, almond butter or cacao.

When making smoothies, you want a really a thick but smooth mixture. So, to get a really "smoothilicious" smoothie and save you from smoothie-fails, use the 60/40 formula. The 60/40 formula is simply 60% fruit to 40% leafy greens. The great thing about the NutriBullet is that it is exceptional well suited for making smoothies with the perfect texture.

Begin making your smoothies by using your NutriBullet to blend your leafy greens with the liquid-base. Next, add in your fruit and blend again. If you want even more nutrients, use less ice and replace it with a frozen fruit. If you enjoy a sweet tasting smoothing you can sweeten it up by using naturally sweet fruits. This way you avoid artificial sweeteners and processed sugars.

Even though smoothies are delicious and healthy, they are extremely convenient. Smoothies are an excellent "on the go" food that can be made the night before and stored in the refrigerator. Simply shake them up right before you're ready to drink them and enjoy!

I sincerely hope you enjoy making and drinking these smoothies as much as my family and I do.

All the best,

Ashley

P.S. For some additional juicing recipes visit:
http://www.deepthoughtpress.com/nutribullet/

PREVENTION SMOOTHIES

Banana Ginger Smoothie

A natural, soothing remedy for digestion, heartburn, nausea and other stomach trouble with fresh ginger. Ginger helps with the reduction of bloating and reduces nausea, especially for the Mom with morning sickness.

Serves: 2

Ingredients:

- 1 banana, sliced
- 6 oz. vanilla yoghurt
- 1 tablespoon honey
- ½ teaspoon grated ginger

Preparation:
Place all the ingredients into the Nutribullet. Blend until smooth and serve.

Nutrition: (per serving)
157 cal, 1g fat, 0.8g sat fat, 57mg sodium, 34g carbs, 28g sugars, 1.5g fibers, 5g proteins

Orange Dream Creamsicle

A tough workout? A hot day at the beach? Then cool off with this low-calorie, citrus-infused smoothie.

Serves: 1

Ingredients:

- 1 navel orange, peeled
- ¼ cup fat-free half-and-half or fat-free yoghurt
- 2 tablespoons frozen orange juice concentrate
- ¼ teaspoon vanilla extract
- 4 ice cubes

Preparation:
Combine the orange, half-and-half or yoghurt, orange juice concentrate, vanilla and ice cubes and process until smooth.

Nutrition: (per serving)
160 cal, 3g protein, 36g carb, 3g fiber, 28g sugars, 1g fat, 0.5g sat fat, 60mg sodium

Green Tea, Blueberry and Banana Smoothie

Antioxidant-rich green tea makes this smoothie a nutritional powerhouse and a cancer-fighting superstar.

Serves:1

Ingredients:

- ½ medium banana
- 1½ cups frozen blueberries
- 2 teaspoons honey
- 1 green tea bag
- 3 tablespoons water
- ¾ cup calcium fortified light vanilla soy milk

Preparation:
In a small bowl, heat the water on high in the microwave until steaming. Add in the tea bag and allow it to brew for 3 minutes and then remove. Stir in the honey until dissolved.
Combine the berries, banana and milk the Nutribullet. Add the tea to the fruit mixture and blend until smooth.
If a smoother drink is required, add in more water. Pour smoothie into a tall glass and serve.

Nutrition: (per serving)
269 cal, 2.5 g fat, 0.2 g sat fat, 52 mg sodium, 63 g carbs, 38.5 g sugars, 8 g fiber, 3.5 g protein

Very Berry Breakfast Smoothie

A fruity, zesty, tangy breakfast smoothie jam packed with health benefits and healing properties.

Serves: 1

Ingredients:

- ¾ cup chilled unsweetened almond or rice milk
- ¼ cup frozen pitted unsweetened cherries or raspberries
- 1 cup frozen unsweetened raspberries
- 1½ tablespoons honey
- 2 teaspoons finely grated fresh ginger
- 1 teaspoon ground flaxseed
- 2 teaspoons fresh lemon juice

Preparation:

Combine all the ingredients adding lemon juice to taste. Puree until smooth. Pour into 2 chilled glasses.

Nutrition: (per serving)
112 cal, 1.5 g fat, 0 g sat fat, 56 mg sodium, 25.5 g carbs, 20 g sugars, 3 g fiber, 1 g protein

World's Best Smoothie

A fulfilling breakfast smoothie that will keep you satisfied until lunchtime.

Serves: 1

Ingredients:

- 1 cup non-fat yoghurt
- ½ cup orange juice
- 1 banana
- 6 frozen strawberries

Preparation:
Place the fruit and yoghurt into the Nutribullet and blend for 35 seconds. Serve immediately.
Nutrition: (per serving)
300 cal, 14 g pro, 63 g carb, 5 g fiber, 45 g sugars, 0.5 g fat, 0 g sat fat, 180 mg sodium

Pineapple Passion

A decadent smoothie island-style smoothie that satisfies the greatest desire for ice cream!

Servers: 1

Ingredients:

- 1 cup low-fat or light yoghurt
- 1 cup pineapple chunks
- 6 ice cubes

Preparation:
Combine the yoghurt and ice cubes in the Nutribullet. Blend for 8-10 seconds.
Add the pineapple chunks and blend until smooth.
Serve in a tall glass topped with a mint sprig.

Nutrition   (per serving)
283 cal, 3.5 g fat, 2 g sat fat, 167 mg sodium, 53.5 g carbs, 48 g sugars, 2 g fibers, 13 g protein

Strawberry-Kiwi Smoothie

Stay sated and fight off disease. This high-fiber drink becomes even healthier when you use organic kiwis, which contain high levels of heart-healthy polyphenols and vitamin C. Enjoy as a morning treat after a strenuous workout or a quick fill-me up if the cravings get to you.

Serves: 4

Ingredients:

- 1 ripe banana, sliced
- 1 kiwi fruit, sliced
- 5 frozen strawberries
- 1¼ cups cold apple juice
- 1½ teaspoons honey

Preparation:
Add all of the ingredients into the Nutribullet and blend until smooth.

Nutrition: (per serving)
87 cal, 0.3 g fat, 0 g sat fat, 3.5 mg sodium, 22 g carbs, 16.5 g sugars, 1.5 g fiber, 0.5 g protein

Banana-Blueberry-Soy Smoothie (BBS)

This is a delicious smoothie bursting with succulent blueberries. Skip the sweetener or sugar or substitute with honey for a healthier pick-me up.

Serves: 2

Ingredients:

- ½ frozen banana, sliced
- ½ cup frozen loose-pack blueberries
- 2 teaspoons sugar or 2 packets artificial sweetener
- 1 teaspoon vanilla extract
- 1 ¼ cups light soy milk

Preparation:
Add 1 cup milk, the banana, blueberries, sugar or sweetener and vanilla extract. Blend for 20 to 30 seconds or until smooth.
Add the balance of the milk if a thinner smoothie is desired.
Serve in a tall glass with a slice of banana on the side.

Nutrition: (per serving)
125 cal, 1.5 g fat, 0.1 g sat fat, 60 mg sodium, 25 g carbs, 11 g sugars, 2 g fiber, 3 g proteins

Tropical Papaya Perfection

A tropical, coconut-infused smoothie, reminiscent of island life, packed with cancer fighting properties.

Serves:1

Ingredients:

- 1 papaya, cut into chunks
- ½ cup fresh pineapple chunks
- 1 cup fat-free yoghurt
- 1 teaspoon coconut extract
- 1 teaspoon ground flaxseed
- ½ cup crushed ice

Preparation:
Combine the fruit, yoghurt, coconut extract, ground flaxseed and ice in the Nutribullet and process until smooth and frosty, about 30 seconds.

Nutrition: (per serving)
299 cal, 1.5 g fat, 0.1 g sat fat, 149 mg sodium, 64 g carbs, 44 g sugars, 7 g fiber, 13 g proteins

Just Peachy

A sinful yet slimming, fat-free vanilla ice cream smoothie packed with taste. Skip the sugar for a healthier alternative.

Serves: 2

Ingredients:

- ½ cup frozen peaches
- ½ cup strawberries
- 2 tablespoons low-fat vanilla yoghurt or fat-free vanilla ice-cream
- 1 cup 1% milk
- ⅛ teaspoon powdered ginger
- 2 teaspoons whey protein powder
- 3 ice cubes

Preparation:
Blend together the milk, yoghurt or ice-cream and protein powder to ensure that the protein powder is evenly distributed. Add in the fruit and lastly the ice. For a thicker smoothie add in more ice which adds volume without adding calories.

Nutrition: (per serving)
150 cal, 2 g fat, 1 g sat fat, 73 mg sodium, 26.5 g carbs, 24 sugar, 9 g protein

Apricot-Mango Madness

A delectably sweet, summer blend with a fresh lemon twist that adds a splash to this any day.

Serves: 2

Ingredients:

- 6 apricots, peeled, pitted and chopped (about 2 cups)
- 2 ripe mangos, 10 – 12 oz. each, peeled and chopped (about 2 cups)
- 1 cup reduced-fat milk or plain low-fat yoghurt
- ¼ teaspoons vanilla extract
- 4 teaspoons fresh lemon juice
- 8 ice cubes
- Lemon peel twists or grated rind (garnish)

Preparation:
Place the fruit, milk or yoghurt, lemon juice and vanilla extract in the Nutribullet. Process for 8 seconds, then add in ice cubes and process until smooth, 6 to 8 seconds.
Pour into tall glasses, garnish with lemon twists or rind, if desired and serve immediately.

Nutrition: (per serving)
252 cal, 3.5 g fat, 1.5 g sat fat, 57 mg sodium, 53 g carbs, 45.5 g sugar, 6 g fiber, 7 g protein

Watermelon Wonder

Summer in a glass, that's what this smoothie is. A light, airy smoothie perfect for summer days to quench that thirst, give you an energy boost without the sugar and calories.

Ingredients:

- 2 cups chopped watermelon
- 2 cups ice
- ¼ cup fat-free milk

Preparation:
Ensure that your use seedless watermelon or remove the seeds before blending.

Add all the milk and watermelon chunks to the Nutribullet and blend until smooth, about 15 seconds, then add in the ice and blend until the desired consistency is reached. Add more ice if needed and blend for about 10 seconds more.

Serve in long glasses.

Nutrition: (per serving)
56 cal, 0.3 g fat, 0 g sat fat, 19.5 mg sodium, 13 g carbs, 11 g sugar, 0.5 g fiber, 2 g proteins

Berry Vanilla Sensation Smoothie

Feeling drained but you need the energy to get your through that gym circuit or the strenuous workout, then this easy-to-make smoothie is the answer. Packed with energy, it will give you the power to pack a punch!

Ingredients:

- 1½ cups chopped strawberries
- ½ cup raspberries
- 1 cup blueberries
- 1 teaspoon fresh lemon juice
- 2 tablespoons honey
- ½ cup ice cubes

Preparation:
Add the ingredients into the Nutribullet and blend till smooth.

Nutrition: (per serving)
162.5 cal,1 g fat, 0.1 g sat fat, 5 mg sodium, 41.5 g carbs, 32 g sugar, 6g fiber, 2 g protein

Tutti-Frutti Smoothie

Power packed with health yet refreshing too. This concoction with a splash of orange juice infuses it with a summery twist. Great for those susceptible to colds and flus.

Serves: 2

Ingredients:

- ½ cup loose-packed mixed frozen berries or strawberries
- ½ cup canned crushed pineapple in juice
- ½ cup sliced banana
- ½ cup plain yoghurt
- ½ cup orange juice

Preparation:
Combine the fruit, including the juice from the pineapple and yoghurt in the Nutribullet and blend until smooth.

Nutrition: (per serving)
140 cal, 2.5 g fat, 1.5 g sat fat, 30 mg sodium, 29 g carbs, 16 g sugars, 2.5 g fiber, 3.5 g protein

Lucy's Luscious Smoothie

An absolute perfect gem if you are diabetic and require a low GI smoothie as the cinnamon reduces cholesterol, regulates the blood sugar levels and boosts the metabolism.

Ingredients:

- 1 cup frozen, unsweetened strawberries
- 1 tablespoon cold-pressed organic flaxseed oil
- 1 tablespoon sunflower or pumpkin seeds (optional)
- 1 cup skim milk

Preparation:
In the Nutribullet, combine the strawberries and milk and blend for a minute. Pour into a tall glass and stir in the flaxseed oil and sprinkle the sunflower or pumpkin seeds over to serve.

Nutrition: (per serving)
256 cal, 14 g fat, 1.5 g sat fat, 106 mg sodium, 26 g carbs, 19 g sugar, 3 g fiber, 9 g protein

Slim-Down Smoothie

A really great substitute for milkshakes and ice cream, thick and wonderfully tasty. Perfect for those idyllic summer days.

Ingredients:

- 1 cup frozen berries – blueberries, strawberries, raspberries
- ½ cup orange juice
- ½ cup low-fat yoghurt (your flavor)

Preparation:
Place the ingredients into the Nutribullet and blend till smooth and serve in a tall glass with a slice of orange as a garnish.

Nutrition: (per serving)
185 cal, 2 g fat, 1 g sat fat, 90 mg sodium, 35 g carbs, 26 g sugar, 3.5 g fiber, 8g protein

Soy, Soy Good Smoothie

When hunger pangs gnaw at your stomach, it is such a soy good time. It's also an excellent mid-morning, on-the-run smoothie.

Serves: 1

Ingredients:
- 1 frozen banana, sliced
- ½ cup frozen blueberries
- ½ cup cornflake cereals
- 1 cup calcium-fortified vanilla soy milk

Preparation:
Combine the fruit, cereal and milk and blend for 30 seconds. Serve.

Nutrition: (per serving)
350 cal, 3.5 g fat, 0.1 g sat fat, 192 mg sodium, 74 g carbs, 44 g sugar, 7 g fiber, 9 g protein

Tropical Mango Madness Smoothie

This antioxidant rich smoothie makes a perfect disease-fighter. It's also great for your hair and skin. Research has shown that mango may help prevent breast cancer.

Ingredients:
- 1 large ripe mango, peeled and chopped
- 8 oz. can juice-packed pineapple chunks
- 1 ripe banana, sliced
- 1 cup fat-free frozen vanilla yoghurt
- Crushed ice

Preparation:
Add the fruit and yoghurt to the Nutribullet and blend until smooth. Add in the ice cubes and blend until the ice is pureed.

Nutrition: (per serving)
251 cal, 0.5 g fat, 0.2 g sat fat, 68 mg sodium, 60 g carb, 50 g sugar, 4 g fiber, 6.5 g protein

SLIMMING SMOOTHIES

Mango Surprise Smoothie

A tropical nectar that is great for those who find it difficult to omit sugar in the beginning stage of a weight loss diet. Give it a try and gradually lessen the sugar. But wait till you feel the energy boost and weight loss too.

Serves: 1

Ingredients:

- ¼ cup mango cubes
- ¼ cup ripe avocado, mashed
- ½ cup mango juice
- ¼ cup fat-free vanilla yoghurt
- 1 tablespoon sugar
- 1 tablespoon freshly squeezed lime juice
- 6 ice cubes

Preparation:
Blend all the ingredients until smooth. Pour into a tall glass, garnish with a strawberry or mint sprig and serve.

Nutrition: (per serving)
298 cal, 9 g fat, 1.5 g sat fat, 54 mg sodium, 55 g carb, 47 g sugar, 5 g fiber, 5 g protein,

Blueberry Smoothie

This bright smoothie is perfect to as a summer midmorning, midday or afternoon snack. Refreshing and energy boosting to get you up and running from a slump.
Serves:1

Ingredients:

- 1 cup frozen unsweetened blueberries
- 1 cup skim milk
- 1 tablespoon cold-pressed organic flaxseed oil

Preparation:
Combine and blend all the ingredients together in the Nutribullet except the flaxseed oil. Pour into a glass and stir in the flaxseed oil. Serve.

Nutrition: (per serving)
273 cal, 14.5 g fat, 1.5 g sat fat, 29 g carb, 24 g sugar, 103 mg sodium, 4 g fiber, 9 g protein

Bano-Peanut Butter Smoothie

An energy boost in a glass kind of smoothie! A distinctive flavor and great taste that is a powerhouse of energy.

Serves: 1

Ingredients:
- ¼ very ripe banana
- 2 tablespoons creamy natural unsalted peanut butter (MUFA)
- ½ cup fat-free milk
- ½ cup fat-free plain yoghurt
- 1 tablespoon honey
- 4 ice cubes

Preparation:
Add all of the ingredients into the blender. Process until smooth. Pour into a tall glass and serve.

Nutrition: (per serving)
366 cal, 16.5 g fat, 3.5 g sat fat, 40 g carb, 151 mg sodium, 32 g sugar, 3 g fiber, 18 g protein

Vanilla and Blueberry Smoothie

A glass of health and nutrition imparting an energy boost and a feeling of well-being with it excellent nutrient content and great taste.

Serves: 1

Ingredients:

- 1 cup fresh blueberries
- 6 oz. vanilla yoghurt (80 calorie)
- 1 cup skim or soy milk
- 1 tablespoon flaxseed oil (MUFA)

Preparation:
Add all the ingredients but the flaxseed oil to the blender and process for 1 minute. Transfer to a glass and stir in the flaxseed oil. Serve.

Nutrition: (per serving)
443 cal, 14.5 g fat, 1.5 g sat fat, 57 g sugar, 63 g carb, 221 mg sodium, 4 g fiber, 18 g protein

Just Peachy Smoothie

Peaches are great as a snack food for losing weight and are rich in phytochemicals. These phenols act as antioxidants which can help fight obesity related diabetes and cardiovascular disease.

Serves: 1

Ingredients:
- 1 cup frozen unsweetened peaches
- 1 cup skimmed milk
- 2 teaspoons cold-pressed organic flaxseed oil (MUFA)

Preparation:
Place the milk and peaches together and blend until smooth. Pour into a glass and add in the flaxseed oil and stir well.

Nutrition: (per serving)
213 cal, 9 g fat, 1 g sat fat, 26 g carb, 103 mg sodium, 22 g sugar, 2 g fiber, 9 g protein

Citrusy Lemon-Orange Smoothie

Oranges contain phytonutrients and Vitamin C, a water-soluble antioxidant that disarms free radicals and preventing damage to the inside and outside of the cell. A good intake of Vitamin C is essential to the reduction of colon cancer. It is also associated with the reduction of severity of inflammatory conditions like asthma, osteoarthritis and rheumatoid arthritis.

Serves:1

Ingredients:
- 1 medium orange, peeled, cleaned and sliced
- 1 cup skim or soy milk
- 6 oz. lemon yoghurt (80-calorie)
- 1 tablespoon flaxseed oil (MUFA)
- Handful of ice

Preparation:
Bring the yoghurt, milk, orange slices and ice together in a blender and process until smooth. Transfer to a glass and stir on flaxseed oil.

Nutrition: (per serving)
420 cal, 14g fat, 1.5 g sat fat, 57 g carb, 54 g sugar, 219 mg sodium, 3 g fiber, 18 g protein

Spicy Apple Smoothie

Phytonutrients contained in apples help prevent spikes in blood sugar and they are also known to lower blood lipids. Apples definitely keep the doctor away and they help you lose weight. They can also help regulate blood sugar for those that suffer with diabetes.

Serves: 1

Ingredients:
- 1 medium apple, peeled and chopped
- 1 teaspoon apple pie spice
- 6 oz. vanilla yoghurt (80-calorie)
- ½ cup skim or soy milk
- 2 tablespoons cashew butter (MUFA)
- Handful of ice

Preparation:
Add all ingredients to the Nutribullet and process until smooth. Transfer into a bowl and eat with a spoon.

Nutrition: (per serving)
482 cal, 16.5 g fat, 3.5 g sat fat, 71 g carb, 300 mg sodium, 5 g fiber, 19 g protein

Tropicalicious Pineapple Smoothie

Pineapples help in the digestion in the intestinal tract and bromelain is an enzyme popular in dietary supplements are found in pines.

Serves: 1

Ingredients:

- 4 oz. canned pineapple tidbits in juice
- 1 cup skim milk
- 1 tablespoon cold-pressed organic flaxseed oil (MUFA)
- Handful of ice

Preparation:
Place the ingredients, except the flaxseed oil, into the blend and blend till smooth. Pour the mixture into a glass and add in the flaxseed oil, stir well. Serve.

Nutrition: (per serving)
271 cal, 14 g fat, 1.5 g sat fat, 30 g carb, 29 g sugar, 104 mg sodium, 1 g fiber, 9 g protein

Strawberry Stunner Smoothie

Not only is this a tasty, refreshing smoothie but it is packed with health benefits including aiding those with diabetes, cancer and arthritis but it is also been a unique factor in anti-aging.

Ingredients:

- 1 cup frozen unsweetened strawberries
- 1 cup skim milk
- 2 teaspoons cold-pressed organic flaxseed oil (MUFA)

Preparation:
Combine the milk and strawberries in a blender and blend till smooth. Transfer to a glass, stir in the flaxseed oil and serve.

Nutrition: (per serving)
216 cal, 9.5 g fat, 1 g sat fat, 26 g carb, 19 g sugar, 106 mg sodium, 3 g fiber, 9 g protein

DETOX SMOOTHIES

Limango Collard Green Smoothie

A smooth, bright green, refreshing smoothie packed with super foods that clean and detox the system whilst providing nutrition.

Serves:1

Ingredients:

- 1¼ cups chopped kale leaves (remove stems and rib)
- 1¼ cups frozen cubed mango
- 2 medium ribs celery, chopped
- 1 cup chilled fresh orange or tangerine juice
- ¼ cup chopped flat-leaf parsley
- ¼ cup chopped fresh mint

Preparation:
Combine the ingredients together in the Nutribullet and process until smooth. Pour into glasses and serve.

Nutrition: (per serving)
160 cal, 0.5 g fat, 0 g sat fat, 39 g carb, 56 mg sodium, 3 g protein

Hale to the Kale

With a definite role in supporting the body's detox process, it has become a regular in smoothies. Imparting an earthy flavor and health-promoting nutrients, it has become a staple in most health smoothie for detox.

Serves: 1 – 2

Ingredients:

- ½ pear
- ¼ avocado
- ½ cucumber
- ½ lemon
- 1 cup kale (packed)
- Handful of Cilantro
- ½ inch ginger
- ½ cup coconut water
- Pure water
- 1 scoop protein powder (hemp, pumpkin or pea)

Preparation:
Place all the ingredients into a blender and blend till smooth. Pour into glasses and serve cold.

Sweet Spirulina Smoothie

With the onslaught of toxic chemicals in our environment, food and drugs we need to continually rid our bodies of these accumulated toxins. Water and some herbs, fruits, etc. have the power to do this whilst imparting great nutritional value to our bodies. Spirulina constitutes a unique combination of phytonutrients like chlorophyll, phycocyanin and polysaccharides help cleanse the body.

Serves: 1 - 2

Ingredients:
- ½ banana
- ¼ avocado
- ½ cup blueberries
- 1 teaspoon spirulina
- ½ cup almond milk
- Pure water
- 1 scoop vanilla protein powder (pumpkin, hemp or pea)

Preparation:
Using frozen fruit will thicken the smoothie. Place the ingredients into the blender and process well. Transfer to glasses and serve.

Chia Chiller Smoothie

Chia seeds are jam packed with healthy omega-3 fatty acids, carbohydrates, protein and fiber as well as antioxidants and calcium. They are easily absorbed by the body and its fiber is vital in helping with detoxing.

Serves: 1 - 2

Ingredients:
- ½ pear
- ¼ avocado
- 1 cup spinach, packed
- 1 teaspoon chia seeds
- ¼ cup coconut water
- 1 cup almond milk
- 1 scoop protein powder (hemp, pea or pumpkin)
- Pure water

Preparation:

Add the ingredients to the Nutribullet and blend well. Serve in tall glasses.

Tangy Tummy Smoothie

Papaya is packed with powerful anti-oxidants that help bind cancer-causing toxins in the colon which keeps them away from healthy colon cells. Vitamin C and beta-carotene help in reducing inflammation and also strengthens the immune system.

Serves: 1 - 2

Ingredients:
- 1 cup papaya
- 1 cup coconut kefir, yoghurt or cultured coconut milk
- 1 tablespoon raw honey
- Juice from ½ lime

Preparation:
Add the ingredients to the blender and serve.

Smooth Operator

Serves: 1 - 2

Ingredients:

- ½ Granny Smith apple
- ¼ avocado
- ½ cup jicama
- ½ cucumber
- 5 large Romaine lettuce leaves
- Handful of cilantro
- 1 whole lime
- 4 scoops hemp protein
- 1 Medjool date
- Pure water

Preparation:

Prepare the smoothie by placing the ingredients into a blender and blend till smooth. Serve in tall glasses.

Sexy Crazy Goddess

Packed full of vitamins and minerals and tastes so good! This smoothie brings a refreshing, alkalinizing cleanse to the body allowing it to operator optimally.

Serves: 2

Ingredients:

- 1 banana
- 1 avocado, coconut meat, raw almond butter or nut milk
- 1 cup blueberries
- 1 cucumber
- A fistful of kale, romaine or spinach
- Coconut water

Preparation:
Use the Nutribullet to blend all the ingredients together until smooth.

The Sicilian Smoothie

An absolute hearty but spicy smoothie that helps the heart, lowers blood pressure, and relaxes the smooth muscles in the arteries.

Serves: 1 - 2

Ingredients:

- 6 carrots
- 2 red bell peppers
- 3 large tomatoes
- 4 stalks celery
- 1 cup watercress
- 1 cup spinach, loosely packed
- 4 cloves garlic
- 1 red jalapeño, seeded (optional)

Preparation:
Prep the vegetables by washing and drying well. Juice all the ingredients in the Nutribullet. Serve.

Lemon-Blueberry Smoothie

A great smoothie that helps boost immunity. This simple recipe caters for vegans, raw food enthusiasts and vegans too.

Serves:1

Ingredients:

- 1 cup alkaline water
- 1 organic whole lemon
- ¼ cup organic blueberries

Preparation:
Blend all the ingredients in the Nutribullet and serve in a tall glass.

Gingery Blueberry

Ginger adds a special flavor and zest to this smoothie but more essentially possesses a number of therapeutic properties which inhibit the formation of inflammatory compounds, assists in gastrointestinal distress such as vomiting, morning sickness and motion sickness.

Serves:1

Ingredients:

- 1 frozen banana
- ¼ cup blueberries
- 1 cup almond milk or a milk of choice
- 3 tablespoons ginger juice

Preparation:
Blend the ingredients together and serve.

Apple Mint Berry Smoothie

A refreshing combination and a great pick me up that makes an awesome treat. Even the kids will enjoy this one.

Serves: 1 - 2

Ingredients:

- ½ green apple
- ¼ cup organic fresh or frozen berry blend
- 3-4 leaves organic green leaf lettuce
- 8 fresh mint leaves
- 2 tablespoons Manitoba Harvest Hemp Hearts
- 8 – 12 oz. pure water

Preparation:
Place all the ingredients into a blender and blend till smooth. Serve in a tall glass.

Sensual Detox Smoothie

A detoxing and cleansing treat that tastes great leaving you feeling sensual and sexy.

Serves: 1 - 2

Ingredients:

- 4 – 5 red endive leaves
- ¼ cup organic fresh or frozen dark red cherries
- 2 tablespoons hemp seeds
- 1 tablespoons Essential Living Foods cacao powder
- Pinch of Essential Living Foods green stevia
- 8 – 12 oz. pure water

Preparation:
Blend all the ingredients together until smooth. Serve.

Lean Green Machine

Containing chlorophyll, a natural detoxifier helps the intestine to rid itself of stored toxins. The antioxidants found in barley grass are also known to protect cells against toxic free radicals thus assisting aging.

Serves: 1 - 2

Ingredients:
- 1 green apple
- 1 lemon
- 1 cucumber, peeled
- 3 – 4 leaves red leaf lettuce
- ¼ cup organic fresh or frozen mango
- 1 teaspoon Essential Living Food barley grass juice powder
- 8 – 12 oz. pure water

Preparation:
Add all the ingredients to the Nutribullet and blend until smooth. Serve cold. Enjoy.

Glowing NutriBlast

Magnesium, a potent defense against migraines and improvement in sleep, is found in pumpkin seeds, making this smoothie a tonic for those with insomnia and migraines.

Serves:1

Ingredients:

- 1 pear, cored and seeded
- 1 lemon, peeled
- 1 orange, peeled
- 25% spinach
- ½ cucumber
- 1 tablespoon pumpkin seeds
- Water

Preparation:
Blend the ingredients in Nutribullet, adding water to the max line. Blend and serve.

Warrior Tonic

An energizing smoothie that allows one to gain stamina for those long workouts and exhausting days. The mace, chia and lucuma provide the nutrients required for this with the fruit and cacao complimenting them.

Serves:1

Ingredients:

- 1 tablespoon lucuma powder
- 1 – 2 tablespoon maca powder
- 2 tablespoons chia seeds
- 1 – 2 tablespoons cacao nibs
- 1 scoop vanilla protein powder
- 1 organic ripe banana
- 1 tablespoon coconut oil
- 1 cup almond milk

Preparation:
Blend the ingredients together and serve in a tall glass.
Nutrition:

Clear Skin Sip

Coconut restores radiance and moisturizes, whilst parsley oxygenates, cucumber revitalizes, lime with its vitamin C content provides toning and the vitamin A in mint helps strengthens skin tissue and reduces oily skin, making this smoothie an excellent source of goodness to the skin and fighting of aging.

Serves:1

Ingredients:

- 1 cucumber
- 1 lime
- 1 apple
- ½ cup flat-leaf parsley (packed)
- 2 tablespoons fresh mint leaves
- 1 cup coconut kefir
- 1 tablespoon coconut oil

Preparation:
Blend all the ingredients together in a Nutribullet. Serve with a sprig of mint.

The Fountain of Youth

Chock full of protein and amino acids and a great alkalizer. Drink up if you want to keep those cells plump thus a glowing, radiant skin.

Serves:1

Ingredients:

- 1 – 2 green apples
- 3 stalks of kale
- Handful of spinach
- ½ cup cilantro (leaves and stems)
- ½ cup flat-leaf parsley (leaves and stems)
- ¼ teaspoon fresh grated ginger
- 1 – 2 heaped tablespoon wild blue-green algae
- 1 cup coconut water

Preparation:
Blend and enjoy.

Cranberry Cleanser

The perfect winter detoxifier that helps the kidneys to cleanse itself giving the body a one-up on the health scale.

Serves: 1

Ingredients:

- 1 large celery stalk
- 1 cucumber
- 1 apple
- 1 pear
- ½ cup cranberries
- Handful spinach

Preparation:
Put all the ingredients into the blender and pulse until smooth. Serve.

"Fat Flush" Juice

Looking to have a flatter belly and detoxing to achieve optimal health, then this is the smoothie for you. Jam packed with nutrients and antioxidants, it helps to cleanse whilst imparting much needed nutrients.

Serves: 1

Ingredients:

- 3 medium organic carrots
- 1 medium organic red beet
- 1 organic radish
- 2 organic garlic cloves
- Large handful organic parsley

Preparation:
Blend all the ingredients together until smooth. Pour into glasses and sip.

Simply Healthy

Peachy Watermelon Smoothie

Packed full with some of the most powerful antioxidants, including Vitamin C, A and B7 which help reduce the chances of colon cancer and relieves the symptoms of osteoarthritis and rheumatoid arthritis. Say cheers and enjoy the health benefits.

Serves:1

Ingredients:

- 1 cup frozen strawberries
- 2 – 3 cups watermelon chunks, seeded
- 6 oz. low-fat vanilla yoghurt
- ½ cup peach juice or 1 peach

Preparation:
Blend all the ingredients together and serve in tall glasses with a slice of strawberry to garnish.

Nutrition: (per serving)
306 cal, 3.2 g fat, 58.0 g carb, 48.7 g sugar, 5.0 g fiber, 13.6 g protein

Good Morning Green Smoothie

The color and taste of this power packed, energy boosting smoothie catches the senses and it does not disappoint in its reputation of being full of healthy and energy. Grab a glass and get a health and energy boost.

Serves:2

Ingredients:

- 1 cucumber
- 2 Romaine leaves
- 2 handfuls of spinach
- 2 stalks celery
- 1 orange
- 1 cup blueberries
- ½ apple
- 3 strawberries
- ¼ squeezed lemon
- ¼ cup pomegranate juice

Preparation:
Blend the ingredients in the Nutribullet till smooth. Serve garnished with a julienned strip of celery.

Nutrition: (per serving)
338 cal, 1.7 g fat, 83.6 g carb, 52.4 g sugar, 16.7 g fiber, 7.0 g protein

Winter Smoothie

Serves: 2

Ingredients:

- ½ avocado
- ½ small frozen banana
- ½ cup frozen blueberries
- A handful baby spinach or kale
- 1 tablespoon cocoa powder
- 1 tablespoon raw honey
- 2 cups water
- Pinch of Cayenne

Preparation:
Using the Nutribullet blend all the ingredients except the cayenne. Pour into glasses and garnish with the Cayenne pepper. Enjoy.

Nutrition: (per serving)
188 cal, 10.5 g fat, 23.2 g carb, 16.2 g sugar, 6.3 g fiber, 2.5 g protein

Heart Healthy Smoothie

The ingredients ensure that this is a low cholesterol, low sodium, high in manganese and vitamin C packed smoothie is a salve for the heart muscle, giving strength and nourishment.

Serves: 2

Ingredients:

- 1 cup fresh or frozen strawberries
- ½ medium banana
- ¼ cup raw almonds
- ½ cup rolled oats
- 3 oz. low-fat vanilla yoghurt
- 1 teaspoon maple syrup

Preparation:
Place the ingredients in the blender and process for about 45 seconds. Pour into glasses and serve.

Nutrition: (per serving)
499 cal, 15.7 g fat, 73.8 g carb, 30.8 g sugar, 11.6 g fiber, 17.4 g protein

Minty Lemon and Honeydew Melon Smoothie

Honeydew melon is great in a smoothie as it is low in calories as it has a high volume of water and fiber. Great to use if you are on a detoxing diet or one for weight loss.

Serves: 2

Ingredients:

- 1½ cups diced honeydew melon
- 1 cup frozen green grapes
- ½ cup non-fat lemon yoghurt
- 1 tablespoon chopped fresh mint
- Fresh lemon juice to taste (optional)

Preparation:
Begin by combining the honeydew and lemon yoghurt in the blender. Add in the grapes and mint and process until smooth. Taste and season with lemon juice if desired.

Nutrition: (per serving)
228 cal, 7 g fat, 64.1 g carb, 53.9 g sugar, 3.5 g fiber, 9.2 g protein

Nutmeg Spiced Honey Banana Smoothie

Hmmmm, sounds like heaven and tastes like it to. Not only does it get the taste buds talking but the other body parts will love it to.

Serves: 2

Ingredients:

- 1 ripe frozen banana, diced
- 6 oz. low-fat natural vanilla yoghurt
- 8 oz. cold milk, low-fat or soy
- 1 – 2 teaspoons honey
- ⅛ teaspoon nutmeg
- A few ice cubes, for a thicker consistency

Preparation:
Begin by adding the liquid to the blender, then the yoghurt and finally the solids. Blend until smooth. Pour into glasses and flavor the honey and nutmeg. Add more ice cubes if you prefer a thicker consistency.

Nutrition: (per serving)
344 cal, 4.8 g fat, 56.2 g carb, 44 g sugar, 3.1 g fiber, 18.7 g protein

Spiced Pumpkin Smoothie

Pumpkin helps in improving eyesight, aids in weight loss, helps reduce the risk of cancer, protects the skin, boosts the immune system and provides energy. So grab a glass of this spiced concoction and begin the journey to health.

Serves: 2

Ingredients:
- 1/3 cup pure pumpkin puree
- ½ cup whole milk
- 1 tablespoon honey
- 1 cup ice
- Pinch of ground nutmeg

Preparation:
In a blender, place the ice, milk, pumpkin puree, honey and nutmeg. Blend until smooth and frothy. Serve with a sprinkling of nutmeg in tall glasses.

Nutrition: (per serving)
165 cal, 4 g fat, 29 g carb, 26 g sugar, 53 mg sodium, 3 g fiber, 5 g protein

Other Books by the Author

Dump Cake Recipes
http://www.deepthoughtpress.com/dumpcakes

This is a unique recipe book because it is full of recipes that are very easy, but don't sacrifice flavor and presentation. Gone are your days of cleaning up multiple mixing bowls and splattered electric beaters. Most of these recipes require very minimal dishes and equipment, and some even require only one dish – your cake pan! These well-loved cobbler style cakes gained popularity because of their simplicity and wonderfully gooey texture. Kids and adults alike enjoy the easy 'dump and munch' process.

Easy Mason Jar Recipes
http://www.deepthoughtpress.com/easy-mason-jar-recipes

This collection of fifty easy to prepare and delicious Mason jar recipes can be used to make homemade holiday gifts, entertain guests, or even prepare lunches for the week.

Additional Resources

Skinnylicious Cooking
http://www.deepthoughtpress.com/skinny

I'll teach you how to make allergy-friendly, fat-burning meals taste better than your favorite restaurant foods, all while you never count a single calorie again!

Juicing For Fat Loss
http://www.deepthoughtpress.com/fat-loss-juicing

Learn how over 8,000 people have lost over 25 lbs in just 10 days with the "Juicing for Fat Loss" system. This program gets results and is endorsed By Joe Cross, a celebrity and star of the groundbreaking film "Fat Sick and Nearly Dead." Click here to learn how you can lose weight too.

The Smoothie Diet
http://www.deepthoughtpress.com/smoothie-diet

Lose 20 Lbs in just 5 Weeks! Lose weight, get healthy, and take back the life you deserve. Click here to learn more.

Ezjuice Juicing Software
http://www.deepthoughtpress.com/ezjuice

This amazing new juicing software instantly cranks out healthy juice recipes from the ingredients you already have in your kitchen so you can increase your energy, add anticancer fighting agents to your diet, and lose weight. Click here to get your copy today.

CPSIA information can be obtained at www.ICGtesting.com
Printed in the USA
LVOW04s2022110115
422398LV00033B/2001/P